Communication

contents

A letter from the Author

Hello!

Welcome to **Communication**. *There are lots of ideas here – and they're all about communication. That's an important topic for all of us. The world needs good communicators.*

Of course, there are lots of different types of communication. We can communicate through words, through music, through art and through different languages, to mention just a few. People from different cultures often communicate in different ways. That's part of the fun of learning a foreign language, to find out more about different cultures (and your own).

We're going to look at the language of computers, and also at a special kind of English – 'teen speak'. In many countries, teenager and adult language are different from each other. In fact, it is sometimes difficult for adults to communicate with teenagers!

We'll also take a look at English round the world, and ask why there are different varieties of it. We'll investigate one alphabet – why is it Roman? We'll find out about sending secret messages, and about other forms of communication. Music, flowers, and texting – they're all different ways to send or receive messages.

Finally, let's not forget animals: they can communicate too. Communication is not just for humans!

At the end of every article, there is a CHECKOUT SPOT with further ideas and mini-projects for you to do. And, of course, a whole page of bigger projects to do with your friends or alone.

We really hope you'll enjoy reading and using this Topics title.

Susan Holden

TO THE **TOPICS** USERS

VOCABULARY You can find the key vocabulary for every article in the **WORD FILE** on that page. The pictures will also help you to guess the meaning in context. There is a summary of useful vocabulary on the **Check it out** page. Finally, you can use the *Macmillan Essential Dictionary* to consolidate the new vocabulary.

WEBSITES There is a list of useful website addresses on page 2. Remember that websites change. Be selective!

Check it out

Verbs

Using the senses

hear	listen	point	see
talk	tell	touch	watch

Using visual symbols

draw	read	type	write

Using machines

film	photograph	record

Using movement and gestures

bow	dance	hug	kiss
mime	nod	play	shake hands
shake your head		wave	

Verbal communication

chat	shout	sing
speak	spell	summarise
talk	translate	whisper

Facial communication

frown	laugh	smile	wink

Computers

Nouns

cursor	hard disk	keyboard
modem	mouse	screen

Verbs

blog	chat	key in
log off/on	search	surf

Phones, radio & T.V.

camera-phone	mobile	computer
C.D.-player	desktop	discman
D.V.D.-player	laptop	palmtop
phone	radio	T.V.
video player	walkman	web-cam

Telephones

Nouns

answering machine	button	cellphone 🇺🇸
code	line	mailbox 🇺🇸
message	mobile 🇬🇧	number
prefix	receiver	screen
voicemail 🇺🇸		

Verbs

answer	call (back) 🇺🇸
dial	phone (back) 🇬🇧
reply	return a call

Adjectives

busy 🇺🇸	engaged 🇬🇧

Sources and Resources

We consulted a lot of sources for 'Communication': people, books and the Internet. If you want to find out more about any of the topics, here are some useful Internet sites. Add your own favourite sites and other useful resources.

Humour: www.snoopy.com
Gestures and behaviour: www.cyborlink.com
Alphabet history: www.historian.net/hxwrite.htm
Inventions: http://inventors.about.com/library/bl/bl12.

These words look easy, don't they? We say them when we're greeting someone. But what about the other things? Gestures. Behaviour. Do you touch the other person? Do you stand very near to them? It all depends... on what? On age, on relationships, on culture, on the situation. In fact, the way we greet other people gives them information about ourselves.

Kissing

In some cultures, only friends kiss. In others, it's polite to kiss strangers. O.K. – you just have to notice what other people do. But there are other things to notice, too. How many times? In some areas, one kiss is normal. In others, two. And in really friendly places – three kisses! Then, of course, there's the question of "Where to begin?". On the right, or on the left? Get that wrong, and your noses will bump! Kissing is a nice way to greet someone, but it's not so easy, after all. NOTE: And in Paris – it's four times!

Hugging

This is like kissing – it's important to get it right! In some cultures, like Russia, close physical contact is important. In others, you only hug your best friends. In fact, in some cultures, people stand at quite a distance from each other. They don't touch. They certainly don't hug the other person!

Shaking hands

Adults do this with other adults. It's formal. But how formal? Well, that depends. In France, students often shake hands with older people, like their teacher.

Bowing

Bowing indicates social position. In many societies, it's only done in extreme situations. For example, if you meet royalty, or the president. But in Japan, Thailand and India, bowing is part of normal greeting. And it has its rules, too. Who bows first? How low do you bow? Do you do anything special with your hands, as in India?

Rubbing noses

Here's a greeting we associate with just two cultures - the Inuit and Maoris. Do they really greet each other this way? What are the rules?

Don't forget!

Good communication is often more than just choosing the right words. Gestures and behaviour send messages, too. These non-verbal signals can communicate a lot of extra things. You'd better learn this language!

WORD FILE

bow (v)	To bend your body when you greet someone.
bump (v)	To hit part of your body against something.
formal	Ceremonial; not relaxed.
gesture	A movement of the body.
greet (v)	To say "hello" to somebody.
physical contact	Touching somebody.
relationship	The way in which people are connected socially.
social position	A person's place in their society.
stranger	A person whom you do not know.

behavior   behaviour

How many ways of greeting people can you think of in your culture? Divide them into verbal and non-verbal. Who uses them? In what context? Are there any rules for them?

Computer

Computers are a key part of modern communication.
When you use a computer, English is very useful.
Do you know why? One reason is because English
is an international language.
We can use a computer to communicate in a lot of
different ways. Here are some of them.

E-mails

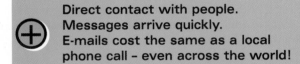

⊕ Direct contact with people.
Messages arrive quickly.
E-mails cost the same as a local
phone call – even across the world!

⊖ It's easy to reply too quickly, before
you think.
* Reflect before you mail!
If commercial companies know your
e-mail address, they can send you
junk mail.
* Only give your address to your friends.

 You'll need a service provider (ISP)
and an e-mail address.

Chat rooms such as ICQ or Messenger

⊕ Immediate communication: it's like
writing a phone call!
You can meet lots of new people.
There are hundreds of 'special
interest' discussion groups.

⊖ You have to type quickly!
Some of the groups are very strange.
* It's important not to give your
personal information.
(See page 6 for some chat room tips.)

 You'll have to register with a Chat Room
host, such as ICQ or Messenger. They'll
ask you for a personal codename to
log on: don't forget it!

WORD FILE

codename	A name to hide your real name.
consult (v)	To ask for information or advice.
discussion group	A group of people who discuss a specific subject.
host	A company that organises a website.
ICQ (I Seek You)	A free-of-charge international website server.
ISP	Internet Service Provider: a company that connects you to the Internet.
junk mail	Information by mail, or e-mail, that you do not want.
log on (v)	To connect to the Internet.
personal information	Information about you.
search engine	A computer programme to find information on the Internet.
special interest	A group of people with an interest in one topic.

Surfing the Internet

⊕ There's a lot of information available. It's
like a huge library. You don't have to leave
your room, or consult lots of books. Most
of the information is free!

⊖ There's so much information that you can
get lost! You can spend a lot of time finding
a good website.

 Find a good search engine to help you.

chat

Google

Search engines such as **Google**

They help you to find specific addresses quickly. It's easy to find information: you type in your topic, and you get a list of possible addresses. They're very quick to use. They're free.

Some of the websites are bad, or old, or not relevant to you. Sometimes it's difficult to find the most useful address.

Some of these websites include lots of ads. These are often pop-ups and they are often very distracting.

E-commerce

You can buy things without going out. Prices are often lower when you buy on-line. Your purchases are delivered to your house: no need to carry heavy bags!

You can't see the real thing before you buy it. You can't try clothes on, so they may not be the right size for you. It's easy to buy things you don't need!

Make sure your credit card details are secret.

Blog

This is a nice way to record your thoughts every day. It is a kind of interactive diary. You can read other people's ideas, and comment on them. Some blogs have links to an archive, or to other website addresses.

It's important to find a good blog: there are lots of bad ones.
When you create a blog, you have to update it every few days. Lots of work!

Some blogs use web-cams to show pictures of the bloggers. Some people use blogs to discuss private topics.
(See the Safe Surfer advice on page 6.)

WORD FILE

archive	Computer files from the past.
blog (biographical log)	A personal diary on the Internet.
blogger	A person who writes a blog.
on-line	Connected to a computer.
pop-up	A small computer screen, usually with advertising.
record (v)	To remember something by writing it down.
relevant	Important and connected to a specific topic.
try on (v)	To put on clothes to check how they look.
update (v)	To add new information.
web-cam	A camera connected to a computer.

Show me mail from:

Everyone

What are your favourite ways of using a computer?
What are the plus and minus points?
Do other people have the same opinions?

SAFE SURFING

THE INTERNET'S GREAT...

For many people, chat rooms are part of modern life. They're a great way of communicating, of meeting new people, and of exchanging information.

There can be unexpected problems, though, and it's wise to be a Safe Surfer. Here are a few tips from a website.

Careful! Who are you talking to?
- Chat rooms and message boards are fun, but they can also be dangerous. You can't be sure who you're talking to
- When you register or join a chat room, tell a 'trusted adult' about it.

Don't give out your personal information.
- Keep these things secret: your full name, address, phone numbers (home and mobile), e-mail address, school name and friends' personal details. Remember! People can use this information to contact you

If you feel worried or uncomfortable, tell an adul
- Some message boards have an 'alert' button. Use this to te the host if something worries you.
- Tell a 'trusted adult' if you are worried.
- Remember: you can always log off and leave the website!

Never meet up with a web pal.
- Even if you're curious about them, don't arrange to meet!
- If you **really** want to meet somebody, tell a parent or teac where you are going. Don't go alone!

Don't open junk mail.
- If you give your email address, some websites will try to sell things to you, through junk mail. This is called *spamming*. Don't open these messages. Don't reply.
- Delete messages from people you don't know. If you see something unpleasant, tell an adult.

...BE A SAFE SURFER, AND AVOID STRANGER DANGER!

WORD FILE

alert button	A computer key to press when there is a problem in a chat room.
alone	Without anyone with you.
(be) curious	Wanting to find out something.
host	A company that organises a website.
join (v)	To become a member of a group or a club.
junk mail	Information by mail, or e-mail, that you do not want.
log off/on (v)	To connect to/disconnect from the Internet.
message board	A place where you can write e-mail messages for people in your group.
pal	(slang) A friend.
register (v)	To give your name to a computer company.
spamming	Sending messages to a lot of people on the Internet.
stranger	A person who you do not know.
trusted adult	An adult who you can have confidence in.
unexpected	Surprising.
unpleasant	Not nice.
worry (v)	To feel nervous when there is a problem.

🇺🇸 cellphone   🇬🇧 mobile

Can you suggest any more tips for safe surfing?

Look at this... You can send text messages to your friends on your mobile. But it has a very small screen, so it's a good idea to make your messages short. You can use a kind of code.

TXT THAT MSG!

Text-messaging is a cool way to communicate in writing. It uses the alphabet and numbers to represent the sound of the words. It's good for facts and information, but it's not so good for complex ideas.

> THIS IS 4 U!

> TK U!

> U R A WINNER!

Here are some longer examples of text messages from a teens magazine. They are written by different people. Can you understand them?

(Answers on page 2)

> IF I RULED DE WORLD ID GIVE DE IRAQ PPL EVRYTHING DEY NEED 2 GET BACK 2 A NORMAL LIFE.

> I FINK DAT BEYONCE IS DA BEST! SHE'S A GR8 SINGA.

> I WOZ BORED SO I PRETENDED 2 TALK 2 SUM1 ON MY FONE. BUT THEN MY MOBY RANG!

In some countries, schools don't permit texting in the classroom. In fact, phones and pagers are often completely banned on the school premises.

Another big question: is texting bad for students' writing? Some teachers and parents say that texting is bad for spelling. Others say that it's fun and can motivate students who don't like writing.

What do you think?

WORD FILE

ban (v)	To say that people cannot do somethin'
code	A secret way of writing.
complex	Difficult to understand.
school premises	The buildings and the outside.
screen	The glass 'window' where you see messages on a computer or mobile.
spelling	The correct way to write a word.

Write a Texting Guide. Include the words on this page.

Non-verbal communication: using the senses

Normally, we communicate through language. We use speaking and writing to do this, choosing the most appropriate words for our purpose. We use different senses to send and receive these messages: sight for written messages or sound for spoken communication.

There are other ways of using sound to communicate, of course. Have you ever been on a ship when they practise for an emergency? The international signal for this is three short blasts on a whistle. This sound means "Stop whatever you are doing! Go to the special meeting place quickly. Wait there for instructions. Don't panic!" The sound of the whistle says all this.

In the same way, bells or sirens are used in buildings to signal a fire alarm. No words, but the message is clear. Then there are ambulance bells and police sirens. Mobile ringtones and the signature tunes for T.V. programmes both send us messages without words.

As well as sound, there's *visual* communication: pictures, signs, logos. Very often, these are excellent ways of communicating information, or instructions. A special advantage of them is that they are often international. Global communication is easy through pictures!

Music is another form of international communication. Of course, it can be written down – musicians *read* music – but most people listen to it. It can express emotions and communicate these to other people. Anger, love, excitement – the sound carries the message.

Music can also make us feel part of a group. Go to a public place, like a mall or a shop, and listen to the music. Is it making you feel relaxed or excited? How about the other people there? Will you stay there a long time and buy lots of things? Listen carefully next time you go shopping!

ALSO: Look at the symbols on pages 4 and 5. They indicate 'Plus points', 'Minus points' and 'Watch out!'. Symbols can save space, can't they?

Make a list of all the non-verbal communication you have heard or seen today. How effective is each one? Give each example 1-5 stars (5 = excellent).

WORD FILE

appropriate	Right for a specific situation.
blast	A loud, sudden sound that is unexpected.
emergency	A sudden situation which involves danger.
panic (v)	To have a sudden feeling of fear.
ringtone	The noise that a mobile makes.
sense	A natural ability to see, touch, speak, smell or hear.
sight	The ability to see.
signature tune	The special music for a T.V. programme.
siren	A loud sound on a police car.
whistle	A metal object that you blow into to make a sharp sound.

	practice		practise
	program		programme

Non-verbal communication: gesture and body language

Let's get back to person-to-person communication. We use our bodies, too. Many gestures are useful to reinforce, or even replace, words. But be careful: like words, their meaning is not always clear!

Facial expressions

We often express our feelings through our faces. Can you guess what these people are feeling?

Raising eyebrows

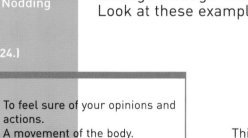

Tap head

Wait a minute. It's not so easy. In Western Europe, people shake their head (horizontal) to communicate "no" and they nod their head (vertical) when they mean "yes". But, in Greece, it's the opposite. Nodding means "No!".

(Answers on page 24.)

Body gestures

Different cultures use different body gestures, too.

But what about this gesture? What does it mean?

This is an international sign for "Stop!"

It depends where you are! "It's a secret!" [UK] but "Shh! It's dangerous." [Italy]

Body language

As well as facial expressions and body gestures, we often communicate our feelings through our body language. Look at these examples.

This kind of information is important for actors when they are studying a role. It can be useful to all of us, too. If you're going for an interview, make sure your body sends out the right signals. "I feel confident!", "I know how to behave well!", "I enjoy talking to you!".

WORD FILE

(be) confident	To feel sure of your opinions and actions.
gesture	A movement of the body.
horizontal	From side to side.
nod (v)	To move your head up and down.
person-to-person	Direct communication between two people.
reinforce (v)	To make something stronger.
replace (v)	To put one thing in the place of another.
role	The character that an actor plays.
vertical	Up and down.

CHECKOUT SPOT.

Find photos of people in newspapers and magazines. Deduce their feelings from their expressions, gestures, and body language.

Say it with flowers

Flowers are a great way to communicate feelings. So are colours. And then there are more modern ways of sending messages: emoticons. All the pictures below communicate a message, an emotion, or a piece of information. What are they? Use the hints box at the bottom of the page. (Answers on page 24.)
Tip: the answers may be different in different cultures.

Flowers

What ideas or information do these flowers or plants express?

Emoticons and smileys

People often want to send a computer message about their feelings. What can you understand from these faces?

:'-(:-(:-)   :-O

Colours

What emotions do these colours suggest to you? Ask a friend. Does he or she agree?

Note the meanings of colours in your culture. Check with your friends: do they agree with you,

WORD FILE

emoticon	A symbol in a computer message to show your feelings.
emotion	How you feel.
jealousy	A feeling of anger because another person has more than you.
purity	Good moral behaviour.
royalty	Kings, queens and their families.

 color   colour

Hints Box

calm	danger	death
jealousy	purity	"I love you!"
"It's Christmas!"	a funeral	royalty
"I'm sad."	"I'm surprised."	"I'm happy!"
"I'm crying."	"Happy Easter!"	

Mixed messages

Communication isn't always simple, is it? It's easy to misunderstand people. We say or do the wrong thing – and they get offended. Sometimes the words are wrong for the situation, and sometimes the other person just doesn't understand the 'behaviour code'.

There are lots of examples of these difficult situations in the Problem Pages of magazines. Let's look at some of them, and see how they can go wrong.

Look before you speak!

Last Saturday, I went into a shoe shop with my friends to buy some new trainers. There were some horrible ones in the window. I pointed to them and said "Ugh! I don't want anything like that! Who wears those things?"

Just then I saw that my new boyfriend was standing near the window – and he was wearing the same trainers. He looked furious – and he walked out. I don't know what to say to him!

D.S., 14, England

Jokes are dangerous!

On holiday last year, I was near the park with a group of my friends. A car stopped and a woman asked "Where's the secondary school?" For a joke, I gave her the wrong directions. On the first day of term, I realised the woman was our new headmistress. I don't want to meet her again!

L.P., 13, England

Look carefully!

My parents took me to Australia to visit my grandparents. We went to Sydney to see the sights. It was fantastic! I wanted to give my Mum a big hug to say 'thank you'. I ran up to her and squeezed her really hard. Then I looked up, and saw it wasn't her. I don't know who was more embarrassed, me or the woman. Of course, Mum was laughing at me!

E.L., 13, England

Animals' problems

Animals have communication problems, too! In the U.S.A., whale-watching is a very popular sport. On the Pacific and Atlantic coasts, hundreds of people go out in boats every year to see whales. Problem is, these boats (and the tourists) make a lot of noise. And this makes it difficult for the whales to hear each other. So what are they doing about it?

Well, imagine you're in a crowded room, with lots of noise. You want to talk to your friends. So – you speak slowly and clearly. You use pauses between each sentence. You use simple language.

In April 2004, scientists noticed that whales are now doing the same thing as humans. They use lots of pauses between their sounds. And they are 'speaking' more slowly, too! They're clever, aren't they?

What's your worst communication situation? What happened? Could you rescue the situation?

WORD FILE

(be) embarrassed	To feel worried about other people's opinions of you.
headmistress	The female head teacher in a school.
sights	Tourist attractions.
squeeze (v)	To hold something tightly with your hands.
whale-watching	Observing whales from a boat.

🇺🇸	🇬🇧
realized	realised
shoe-store	shoeshop
sneakers	trainers
vacation	holiday

MOM!!!

CHECKOUT SPOT

The story of English

What kind of English do *you* speak? American English? Or British English? Or a different variety?

Question: Why are there different types of English?
Answer: Because of History, Politics and Geography.
Let's find out.

1 From England to New England

In 1620, this group of people sailed from England to North America. Their religion was very important for them, and they wanted to be free to live in their own way. They took the English Bible with them. They spoke English: 17th century English. This was the language of Shakespeare, and many of the words, and the pronunciation, were different from modern English. The eastern part of the continent became an English colony. The language here was English, but it began to change. The immigrants needed new words for the plants and animals there. They often used native American words for these. American English was becoming different from the English in England.

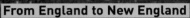

tomahawk · wigwam · moose · Potomac

Whither* goeth thou?

* Where are you going?

2 Independence!

In 1776, after 6 years of war with England, the United States of America became independent. American English continued to develop. And the English-speaking area got bigger and bigger. The French sold Louisiana to the new United States. Spain gave up its colonies in the south. And as English-speaking people from the east coast went west, to look for gold, or to establish enormous cattle ranches, they took the English language with them. They also invented new words for their lives there.

Another influence on American English, of course, was the language of the slaves: Afro-American English. In 1885, Mark Twain's *Huckleberry Finn* used this language in print. "... Aunt Sally she's going to adopt me and sivilize me and I can't stand it."

chutzpah!
gulag **gung-ho**
"I should worry!"

3 Immigration, immigration, immigration

During the 19th and 20th centuries, more and more people went to live in North America. They came from many different countries, and they went there for political, religious or economic reasons. They wanted to start new lives. These new immigrants to North America brought their languages – Spanish, Italian, Chinese, Japanese, Russian, Yiddish – and they all contributed words and phrases to American English.

WORD FILE

cattle ranch	A very big farm for cows.
colony	A country which is controlled by another country.
develop (v)	To change or grow.
establish (v)	To make something begin to happen.
give up (v)	To stop doing something.
immigrant	A person who comes to live in a country.
independent	With its own government.
slave	A person who has to work for another person.
variety	Many different types of something.

4 English travels east

Back in Britain, English was developing too. Politics and trade changed it. During the 18th and 19th centuries, the British Empire grew and grew. People described it as "The Empire where the sun never sets". The soldiers, administrators and traders who built this Empire took English with them. The language travelled to India, to Australia, to Asia, New Zealand and Africa. In many places, it became the language of government.

5 Different Englishes

Britain was a small, overcrowded country, and many people went out to find better lives overseas. They used local words for the new things they found there. Different varieties of English began to develop: Indian English, Singapore English, Australian English. Which one is this?

Once a jolly swagman camped by a billabong
Under the shade of a Coolibah tree...

6 Movies or films?

In the 20th century, because of the invention of the cinema, American English began to travel to Britain. It changed British English. Gradually, speakers of British English became accustomed to hearing American accents. They knew that "sidewalk" and "pavement" were the same thing. The two languages became closer in many ways.

British English has had other influences in the last few years. There is a big immigrant population from India and Pakistan. Asian music and Bollywood movies are very popular among young people – and Asian English is now part of general British "teen speak".

"She looks so Angrez!"

"Don't be so badmash!"

"He's really jungli!"

Listen carefully – there are many different forms of English. It's still developing. The language belongs to the world!
Question: *Which type is correct?*
Answer: *All of them!*
Question: *So... do you speak American English, or British English... or international English?*

7 Still moving!

Films have helped to take American English all over the world. But don't think this is the end of the story. People now speak English all over the world as a first, second, or foreign language. Non-native speakers of English use it as an international language of communication. And people often use English words when they are speaking other languages. French, Spanish, Italian and Portuguese speakers all recognise a "mouse" – which doesn't eat cheese – or a "bug" – which isn't an insect!

CHECKOUT SPOT. Some words are different in the various varieties of English. Do you know any of these? Write a bilingual word list.

WORD FILE

accent	The way people say words in a specific country or region.
administrator	A person who organizes a country or company.
Bollywood	The Indian film industry.
immigrant population	People in a country who have come from a different country.
local	In the area where you live.
overcrowded	A lot of people in a small space.
overseas	In a country across the sea from your country.
set (v)	To establish.
trade (v)	To buy and sell.

🇺🇸 movie	🇬🇧 film
recognize	recognise

Tip: You can check out some examples of British and American English on page 22.

Inventions:

Ways to communicate keep on developing! Let's take a look at some of the most useful inventions. See how every invention results in another development.

TALKING ACROSS DISTANCES

Telephones

Where? The U.S.A.
Who? Alexander Bell (and Thomas Edison).
When? 1876.
Positive points: You can talk to people in different places.
Problems: You can't travel with your telephone!

Mobiles

Where? The U.S.A., Sweden and Japan.
When? The 1970s and 1980s.
Positive points: You can travel with your phone.
Problems: You can't see the other person.

Cameraphones

Where? The U.S.A., Sweden and Japan.
When? Today!
Positive points: You can talk to people in different places AND you can see them!
Problems: Phones are easy to lose. They're easy to steal.

What's next?

What do you think?

Sometimes talking isn't enough. We want to *be* with the other person. We want to have "face-to-face" communication. Technology can help here, too. It's now easy to travel great distances. Air travel is the answer. All you need is time – and money! Let's take a look at some air travel inventions.

What is the most useful invention for helping communication? What are its advantages and disadvantages?

WORD FILE

cameraphone	A mobile that can take photos.
face-to-face communication	Talking to people in the same place as you.
invention	Something which exists for the first time.
steal (v)	To take another person's property.

LET'S GO BY AIR!

For centuries, people dreamed about flying. Do you remember the Greek legend of Icarus? He tried to fly too high, too near the sun, and the wax on his wings melted. He fell into the sea and drowned.

However, in Italy around 1500, Leonardo da Vinci designed a flying machine. How did he do it? He observed birds and worked out the theory of flight. However, he didn't actually *try* his machine!

Of course, some people felt that humans would never fly. But about 300 years later, they did!

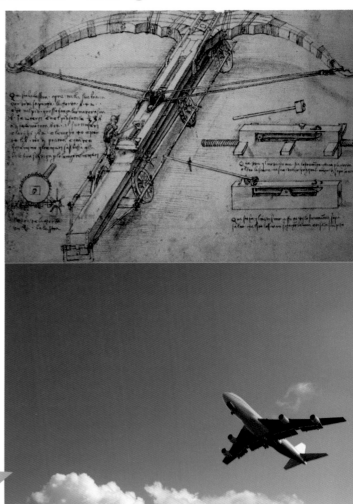

Balloons

Where?	France.
When?	1783.
Who?	The Montgolfier brothers.
Positive points:	People could travel quickly through the air.
Problems:	Journeys depended on the direction of the wind.

The first planes

Where?	France, the U.S.A.
When?	1903.
Who?	Santos-Dumont, the Wright brothers.
Positive points:	The pilot could choose the direction.
Problems:	They were very small. They could not carry passengers for long distances.

Planes

Where?	All over the world.
When?	Today.
Positive points:	They can carry hundreds of people for long distances. Flying is (quite) cheap.
Problems:	Planes pollute the environment. They increase global warming.

What's next?

What do you think?

WORD FILE

dream (v)	To hope to do something in the future.
drown (v)	To die under the water.
flying machine	A machine that can fly.
global warming	The condition of the earth becoming warmer.
legend	An old story.
melt (v)	To become liquid.
theory	Ideas that explain how something works.
try (v)	To experiment with something.
wax	A soft material used to make candles.

 trip   journey

SECRET COMMUNICATION

Sometimes people need to communicate, but the information must be secret. What can they do?

This is a problem, even in the modern world. It is easy to open letters. "Hackers" can intercept e-mails... Telephones aren't safe: there are electronic devices that can "listen in" on conversations. How can you protect your information?

In fact, a *written* message *can* be the answer. But it must be written in a special way – in code. There are lots of different ways to do this. Some of them are very old, and some are new. Here are some examples. Of course, some of them are more useful than others!

A	B	C	D	E	F	G	H	I	J	K	L	M	N	O	P	Q	R	S	T	U	V	W	X	Y	Z
D	E	F	G	H	I	J	K	L	M	N	O	P	Q	R	S	T	U	V	W	X	Y	Z	A	B	C

THE CAESAR CODE
Julius Caesar invented this code around two thousand years ago – and people still use it! Sometimes the simple things are best. You just move all the letters three places to the right, and that's the code.
To decode the message, move them back.
Of course, Caesar used the original Roman alphabet, with 19 letters – see pages 20 and 21! And you can choose a different number of places each time. Just make sure that the other person knows too!

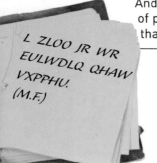

L ZLOO JR WR EULWDLQ QHAW VXPPHU. (M.F.)

ENCRYPTING
What about codes today? In fact, some of them are now a normal part of everyday life. You see, they are used whenever people pay for things by credit card. Individual credit card numbers are turned into a code to keep them secret. Without this system, e-commerce wouldn't be safe.

NUMBER CODES
Here, every letter has a number equivalent. So you send your message in numbers. You must decide how many numbers to use. This one only uses the numbers 0-9.

A	B	C	D	E	F	G	H	I	J	K	L	M	N	O	P	Q	R	S	T	U	V	W	X	Y	Z
0	1	2	3	4	5	6	7	8	9	0	1	2	3	4	5	6	7	8	9	0	1	2	3	4	5

STRANGE... AND TRUE?

LONG HAIR
There is a story that in a battle, long ago, some people shaved a messenger's head, and tattooed a short message on it. Then they waited until the hair grew again. Nobody knew if there was a message there or not!

WORD FILE
decode (v)	To solve a message in code.
device	A machine to do a specific task.
e-commerce	Buying and selling on the Internet.
encrypt (v)	To put information into code.
equivalent	Similar value.
hacker	A person who reads computer programmes illegally.
intercept (v)	To stop something.
listen in (v)	To listen secretly.
safe	Secure.
shave (v)	To remove hair.
turn into (v)	To change into something different.

Either choose one of these codes, or invent your own. Write a message in it. See if your friends can decode it.

CHECKOUT SPOT

Teens Speak

"Teenagers are...!" Adults will probably finish this sentence in one way; teenagers in a different way. Why? Well, communication across generations is often difficult. This seems strange! After all, adults were teenagers themselves once. Perhaps they have short memories. Or perhaps it's because the world is changing so quickly. Being a teenager then, and being a teenager now is different!

It's often easier for a group of teenagers from different countries, with different native languages, to understand each other. Their language relates to their culture: *teenage* culture.

Here's a part of a Teenager English Phrasebook. All the words and phrases come from a teenager magazine. Which ones are new for you? Does this language follow any patterns? Over to you!

Describing things

fab	fabulous (very good)
fave	favourite
funky	unusual
glam	glamorous
gorge	gorgeous
mega-cool	very, very fashionable
nifty	well designed
quirky	strange, individual
sassy	lively and self-confident
yummy	delicious to eat

Things (Stuff)

bling	lots of bright, metallic decoration
clobber	personal possessions
freebie	something free
gear	clothes
moby	mobile phone
pressies	presents
sunnies	sunglasses
trackies	tracksuit

People

bloke	male person
bro	brother
celeb	celebrity
freak	strange person
mates	friends (male and female)
old fogey	old person (adult)
sis	sister

The things people do or are

blinging	wearing bright, flashy clothes
clothes-swap	to change clothes with another person
cringe	to feel embarrassed about something
get hitched	to get married
get the goss	catch up with the gossip
in a strop	in a bad temper
in the buff	naked/with no clothes
savvy	to be smart/know everything

WORD FILE

generation	People who are born in the same period.
pattern	System.

Is there a Teen Speak in your language? Write a phrasebook for foreigners (and adults). Include useful words, phrases and their meanings.

Don't forget the animals

This Topics title is about communication and, so far, all the articles a[re] about human communication. But we're not the only communicators[.] What about the animal world? We all know that animals communicat[e] in very interesting ways. Here are a few examples.

ELEPHANTS

The project

Some film-makers made a special study of elephants in Africa. They disguised their cameras – they looked like dung-heaps – so the animals accepted them. In this way, they were able to film hundreds of hours of the elephants' "private life".

The discoveries

1

Teaching and learning

Older female elephants teach life skills to young ones. These lessons include:

• using a stick to remove flies from their bodies;
• waving branches with leaves to frighten flies;
• using vegetation to scratch their skin;
• playing games with stones, rocks and pieces of wood.

2

Respecting death

When an elephant dies, other elephants often stop by the body for several minutes. They communicate their emotions through their faces, their eyes, their ears, and their bodies. They look sad.

3

Listening with their feet

Elephants can hear sounds from a very long distance. This is because they have special feet. These send low-frequency vibrations to their brains. They can also hear these vibrations through their trunks. The film-makers saw elephants standing and listening with their trunks or their feet.

Why is listening important for elephants? Well, the film-makers think that they want to know where other elephants are. Sometimes they live in small family groups. Sometimes several families live together. And in the wet season, the groups are enormous. So "keeping in touch" is important for them.

WORD FILE	
branch	The 'arm' of a tree.
disguise (v)	To make an object look like something different.
dung-heap	Waste from an animal.
frighten (v)	To make a person feel afraid.
keep in touch (v)	To maintain contact.
life skill	The things that make it easier to survive.
low-frequency	The way a sound wave travels.
private life	The way you live in your family.
remove (v)	To take away.
scratch (v)	To rub a surface of your body.
stick	A thin piece of wood.
trunk	An elephant's long 'nose'.
vegetation	Green plants and leaves.
vibration	A shaking movement.
wave (v)	To move something in the air.
wet season	The months when it rains every day.

Animal communication: having fun

A lot of human and animal communication is for serious purposes. At times, though, it's also for fun. What about animals? Do they play, too?

In 1997, some scientists were working at Pereirinha Beach, in Southern Brazil. There were some dolphins swimming quite near the beach. The scientists saw a small dog going into the water. It swam towards the dolphins. They began to throw the dog into the air. The dog didn't try to escape – it seemed to enjoy the game! This went on for an hour. Then the dog swam back to the beach.

Next day, other dogs swam into the sea in the same place. They tried to play with the dolphins, too!

Scientists are studying the ways in which animals communicate with other animals. However, there is also animal-human communication. Here's another dolphin story. What do you think?

The Institute for Marine Mammal Studies in Mississippi has several dolphins. When people drop paper into their pool, the dolphins take it to their keepers. In exchange for the litter, they receive a fish.

One dolphin, Kelly, does more than this. When she finds litter, she hides it under a rock. Then, when she sees a keeper, she brings a small piece of paper. She gets a fish. She goes back to the rock, and gets another small piece of paper. She receives another fish! And so on! Fun? Intelligence? Or what?

WORD FILE	
drop (v)	To let an object fall to the ground.
escape (v)	To run away from something.
hide (v)	To put an object in a place where nobody can see it.
keeper	A person who looks after animals in a zoo.
litter	Bits of paper which people drop on the ground.
towards	In a specific direction.

How many examples of animal-animal, or animal-human communication can you think of? Which is the most surprising?

CHECKOUT SPOT

From A to Z: the alphabet story

This Magazine uses the Roman alphabet to communicate its ideas through words. Of course, this is not the only alphabet used in the world today. Some other alphabets, like the Russian and Greek ones, also use symbols to represent letters – and many of the letters in the Greek, Russian and Roman alphabets look very similar.

Other languages use ideograms, not letters: a symbol represents a word, or an idea. Many Asian languages use this system: the Japanese alphabet has thousands of ideograms; an educated person needs to learn about 2,000 different symbols (*kanji*) in order to be able to communicate effectively in writing. It's good training for the memory!

On the other hand, most users of the Roman alphabet only need to learn 24-26 different signs. Why is this called a *Roman* alphabet? After all, the Romans wrote in Latin, not English – and they lived in Italy around two thousand years ago. In fact this alphabet goes back even further. It developed because of trade, history and politics. That's why we still use it today.

STEP 1

The Phoenicians
their alphabet: 1800-1000 B.C.

The Ancient Egyptians were very powerful in the East Mediterranean. They used ideograms to write their ideas. Each symbol represented an idea or an object, like many Asian languages today. But, as with Japanese, you need to learn a lot of different symbols. This was a problem for business people and traders: they were in a hurry!

Around 1800 B.C., a clever person lived in Byblos, a port on the Mediterranean Sea. He wanted to write documents quickly in his own language, Canaanite. He chose some of the Egyptian symbols, and decided to link each one with a sound in Canaanite, not with a whole word. That way, he could combine the symbols (letters) to represent words. This was the first true alphabet.

The Phoenicians were sailors and traders. They visited many other countries around the Mediterranean to buy and sell things. They wanted to write down prices, and the names of people and objects. So they used this new alphabet. It was quick and flexible.

The Phoenician alphabet had 22 symbols. These represented the consonants. There were no special symbols for vowels. In this way, the Phoenician language was like written Arabic and Hebrew today.

WORD FILE

clever	Good at understanding things.
combine (v)	To join two or more things.
emigrant	A person who goes to live in a different country.
explorer	A person who looks for new countries.
flexible	Able to move easily.
further	More.
ideogram	A written symbol for an idea or object.
link (v)	To connect.
powerful	Very strong.
price	The cost of something.
symbol	A picture that represents something.
trade (v)	To buy and sell.
training	Teaching to do something.
writing system	The organisation of written text.

🇺🇸 smart	🇬🇧 clever
traveled	travelled

STEP 2

The Greeks
their alphabet: 1000-900 B.C.

The Ancient Greeks travelled in ships, too. Like the Phoenicians, they bought and sold things, and wanted to write down prices. They could use the same symbols for their consonants. But Greek was different from Phoenician. Some sounds did not exist in Greek, so some Phoenician symbols were not useful for them. In Greek, the vowels were important. So the Greeks used these "extra" symbols for their vowels. They also invented some new symbols.

STEP 3

The Romans
their alphabet: from about 600 B.C.

The Roman Empire was very large. The Romans had to communicate with people in distant parts of it, across land and sea. Their language was Latin, but they used many of the letters from the Greek alphabet. The Roman alphabet had 19 letters.

STEP 4

The modern world

The Roman alphabet travelled all over the Roman Empire. Later, it went to the Americas with the Portuguese and Spanish empires. Different languages used it, and added extra letters to represent their special sounds. That's why there are 24 letters in the Portuguese alphabet, and 26 letters in the English one.

This alphabet also travelled to India, South-east Asia and Australia with explorers and emigrants. Today, people all over the world use the Roman alphabet to communicate. Even if they have their own writing systems, they find this alphabet useful for international communication.

Can you find some words in a different alphabet? Perhaps in shop signs, or a restaurant, or in a newspaper. Copy them out. What can you find out about this alphabet? Where does it come from? Do the words go from left to right, or from right to left? Do they go vertically, or horizontally?

Do you know?

(Answers on page 24.)

1. ANIMAL COMMUNICATION

Choose the right verb for these animals. Remember, some animals make more than one sound. And some of them make the same sounds.

bark	cluck	growl	hiss	mew
moo	neigh	purr	quack	roar

Tip: Say the verbs aloud. A lot of them make the noise of the action.

2. COLOUR LINKS

Can you guess the colours? We use one colour twice. Which is it?

1 To be angry	To see ●●●.
2 To be sad	To feel ●●●.
3 An activity can begin	To give the ●●● light.
4 To believe in good things	Every cloud has a ●●● lining.
5 To describe a special day	This is a ●●● letter day.
6 A rainy day	A ●●● day.

3. AMERICAN AND BRITISH ENGLISH

Match the words.

Indoors

1 closet	☐ garden
2 elevator	☐ lavatory
3 faucet	☐ cupboard
4 rest-room	☐ lift
5 yard	☐ tap

Outdoors

1 automobile	☐ chemist's
2 cab	☐ petrol station
3 drug-store	☐ pavement
4 freeway	☐ motorway
5 gas station	☐ shop
6 highway	☐ car
7 movie theater	☐ lorry
8 sidewalk	☐ main road
9 store	☐ cinema
10 truck	☐ taxi

Food and drink

1 candies	☐ crisps
2 chips	☐ chips
3 cookies	☐ sweets
4 French fries	☐ biscuits

Projects

COMMUNICATION POSTER

Make a study of visual communication around your school or house. Look at ads, shop signs, and so on. Take photos, or make notes and drawings. Then make a poster to present these.

COMMUNICATION LOG

Keep a diary for a day (choose a weekend). Note down different pieces of communication under these headings. Then put your feelings under each (use words or emoticons). Look at the model.

TYPE	Action	Feeling
Face-to-face (verbal)	Greeting Mum at breakfast.	"happy"
Face-to-face (non-verbal)	Smiling at Mum.	"very happy"
Written	Writing an E-mail to cousin.	:-(
Sound	Listening to music on CD.	"relaxing"
Visual	Looking at a poster in my room.	"calm"

CODE MESSAGES

Make up a picture code. Write the key and illustrate it. Use it to write secret messages.

COMMUNICATION INVENTIONS

Choose an important invention that helps communication. Research its history. Design a poster to advertise it. Think carefully about the things that you want to emphasise.

ANIMAL OBSERVATION

Choose an animal that you can observe. How does it communicate with other animals, or with humans? Note its movements, sounds and any other features. Present these as a scientific report.

FEELINGS

Choose an emotion (e.g. happy, sad, excited) and design a poster to illustrate this. Use colours, objects, texts – anything that expresses your personal feelings.

PERSONAL ENGLISH WORD BOOK

Keep a notebook with new words and phrases. Mark them American English or British English.

COLOURS OR FLOWERS

Invent your own "language of flowers" or "language of colours". Write a "Dictionary" for it, with pictures.

MUSIC AND LANGUAGE

Choose one of these:
- foreign bands or singers that are popular in your country now;
- songs by singers or groups in your country which are written in English;
- songs written in other foreign languages that are popular now.

Find out all you can about the singers and groups. Play the music and notice the language and the pronunciation. Why are they popular? Write a review for a music magazine to explain this.

 Look at all the things you have checked out in these Spots. Choose the best ones to make a Communication Exhibition with your friends.

Teens chat

Ian: Hi. D'you know any good jokes?

Kirsty: I know some silly ones. What has four legs and only one head?

Ian: Mm... a bed!

Try this. What would you do if you found an elephant in your bed?

Kirsty: Sleep somewhere else!

What's the longest word in the English language?

Ian: No idea!

Kirsty: "Smiled".

Ian: Why'?

Kirsty: There's a mile between the first and last letters!

Ian: OK!

Look at this photo. Can you guess the proverb?

Kirsty: Mm... people whispering secrets - I know: Walls have ears! Don't talk too much - you never know who's listening! Good advice!

Facts Check

Answers

Page 7: If I ruled the world I'd give the Iraqi people everything they need to get back to a normal life. I think that Beyonce is the best! She's a great singer! I was bored, so I pretended to talk to someone on my phone, but my mobile rang!

Page 10: (suggested answers) red = danger; white = purity; green = jealousy; blue = calm; purple = royalty; black = death; 1) holly = Christmas; 2) daffodils = Easter; 3) white chrysanthemums = death; 4) red roses = love;

"I'm crying." "I'm sad." "I'm happy." "I'm surprised.".

Page 16: I WILL GO TO BRITAIN NEXT SUMMER. J.C.

Page 22: 1. ANIMALS COMMUNICATION

cat-mew/purr; chicken-cluck; cow-moo; dog-bark/growl; duck-quack; horse-neigh; lion-roar; snake-hiss;

2. COLOUR LINKS

To see red. To feel blue. To give the red light. Every cloud has a silver lining. This is a red-letter day. A grey day.

3. AMERICAN AND BRITISH ENGLISH

Indoors	5/4/1/2/3
Outdoors	3/5/8/4/9/1/10/6/7/2
Food and drink	2/4/1/3

Can you believe it?

A friend was on holiday.
Where? In Brazil, in the Amazon, four hours away from the nearest city.
She visited an Indian village.
What did she see? This notice for visitors.

English is an international language!

GOODBYE!

We're at the end of 'Communication'. We hope you'll continue to find ways to be a good communicator. See you in the next Topics title. Till then…

Susan Holden